SCHIRMER'S LIBRARY
OF MUSICAL CLASSICS

JOHANN SEBASTIAN BACH

Two- and Three-Part Inventions

For the Piano

Edited by

CZERNY, GRIEPENKERL and ROITZSCH

IN TWO BOOKS
(Also in One Book Complete)

TWO-PART INVENTIONS — Library Vol. 850

THREE-PART INVENTIONS — Library Vol. 851

→ TWO- AND THREE-PART INVENTIONS
(Complete) — Library Vol. 813

G. SCHIRMER, Inc.

Thematic Index

15 Two-part Inventions

15 Three-part Inventions

Fifteen Two-part Inventions.

Johann Sebastian Bach.

Printed in the U. S. A.

cresc.
f
p
cresc.
f
dim.
mf

Allegro moderato. (♩=108)
2.
mf
dim.
p
cresc.
f
mf

dim.
dim.
p
p
p
cresc.
f
tr

Vivace. (♩.=80)
3.
mf
cresc.
f
mf
cresc.
f
(tr
)
(tr
)

decresc.

p poco cresc.

mf

cresc.

f

p

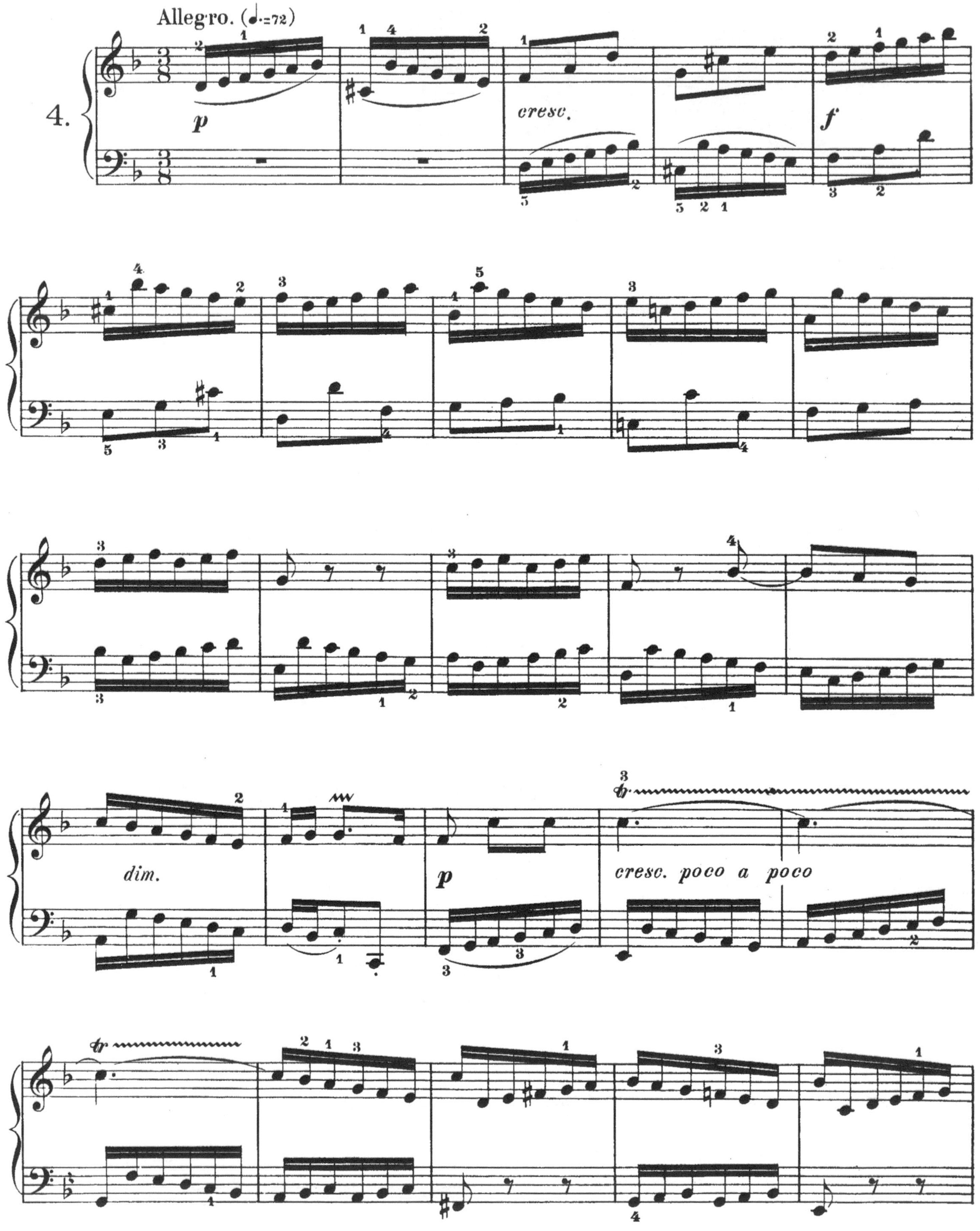
Allegro. (♩.=72)
4.
p
cresc.
f
dim.
p
cresc. poco a poco

f
p
cresc. poco a poco
f
p
cresc.
f
dim.

Allegro moderato. (♩ = 108)
5.
mf
cresc.
f
p
f
p
cresc. poco a poco
f
p

mf
cresc.
p
cresc. poco a poco
f mf
cresc.
f
mf
cresc.
f
p
f

Allegretto. (♪= 144)
6.
p
p
cresc.
f
dim.
p
mf
p
p
p
p

cresc.
f
dim.
p
p
p
cresc. poco a poco
f
p
cresc.

Allegro. (♩= 112)
7.
mf
f
p
cresc.
f
p

cresc.
f
p
cresc.
poco
mf
cresc.
f
p
cresc.
f

Vivace. (♩= 144)
8.
p
f
dim.
cresc.
f
dim.
p
mf

f
f
dim.
cresc.
f
dim.
cresc.
f
dim.

Con spirito. (♩=116)
9.
mf
cresc.
f
mf
cresc.
f
p
cresc.
p
cresc.

p
cresc.
dimin.
mf
cresc.
f
dimin.
p
mf
cresc.
f

Presto. (♩. = 152)
10.
f
poco dimin.
f
p
cresc.
f
mf

cresc.
f
cresc.
ff
dimin.
f

Allegro moderato. (♩ = 108)
11.
p
cresc.
f
cresc.
f

mf
cresc.
f
mf
cresc.
dimin.
p

Allegro giocoso. (♩. = 84)
12.
f
p
cresc.
f
p
cresc.
f
dimin.
f
dimin.
p
legg.
cresc.
f

p
cresc.
f
p
cresc. poco
f
dimin.
f
dimin.
p legg.
cresc.
f
cresc.
f

Allegro tranquillo. (♩= 104)
13.
mf
dimin.
cresc.
f
f
dimin.

decresc. poco a poco
cresc.

Moderato. (𝅗𝅥 = 88)
14.
f
mf
cresc.
f
mf

p
cresc.
f
cresc.
f

Allegro non troppo (♩= 104)
15.
p
mf
cresc.
f
dimin.

p
cresc.
mf
cresc.
f
dimin.
mf
cresc.
dimin.

Fifteen Three-part Inventions.

Printed in the U. S. A.

p
cresc.
f
dimin.
p
cresc.
f

Allegro vivace (♩. = 100)
2.
p
cresc.
f
p
cresc.
f
f

p
cresc.
f
dimin.
p
cresc.
f
dimin.
p
cresc.
f

Allegro moderato (♩= 92)

3.

p

mf

cresc.

f

p

cresc.

f

poco dimin.

p
cresc.
p
cresc.
sf
f
dim.
p
cresc.
f
mf

Allegretto moderato. (♩ = 84)
4.
p
cresc.
f
dim.
p
cresc.
f
dim.
p
cresc.
f

dim.
p
cresc.
f
poco dim.
mf
cresc.
f
dim. poco a poco
p

Allegro moderato. (♩=100)
5.
poco dim.
cresc.
dim.
cresc.
dim.
cresc.

f
dim.
p
poco cresc.
dim.
p
f
decresc.
mf

Allegro moderato (♩. = 84)
6.
p dolce
cresc.
f
dim.
p
cresc.
f

p
cresc.
f
dim.
p
cresc.
f
f
dim. e poco rit.
p

Lento moderato. (♩= 88)
7.
mf
cresc.
f
dim.
p
cresc.
f
dim.

p
cresc.
f
p
f
dimin.

Allegro moderato. (♩= 92)
8.
mf
f
p
cresc.
f
p
cresc.
f

dimin.
p
cresc.
f
p
cresc.
f
mf

Andante espressivo. (♩= 69)
9.
p
cresc.
p
cresc.
f
mf
p
cresc.

f
p
p
cresc.
p cresc.
p cresc.
mf
cresc.
p
cresc.
più cresc.
f
p

Allegretto.
(♩=100)
10.
mf
f
dimin.
p
poco cresc.

f
dimin.
mf
p
cresc.
f
poco dimin.
f

Allegretto moderato. (♩. = 60)
11.
cresc.
dimin.
cresc.
dimin.

cresc.
dim.
dim.
cresc.
dim.

Allegro. (♩= 112)
12.
p
mf
f
dim. poco
cresc.
f
mf
dim.
p cresc.
f

cresc.
dim. poco
cresc.
dim.

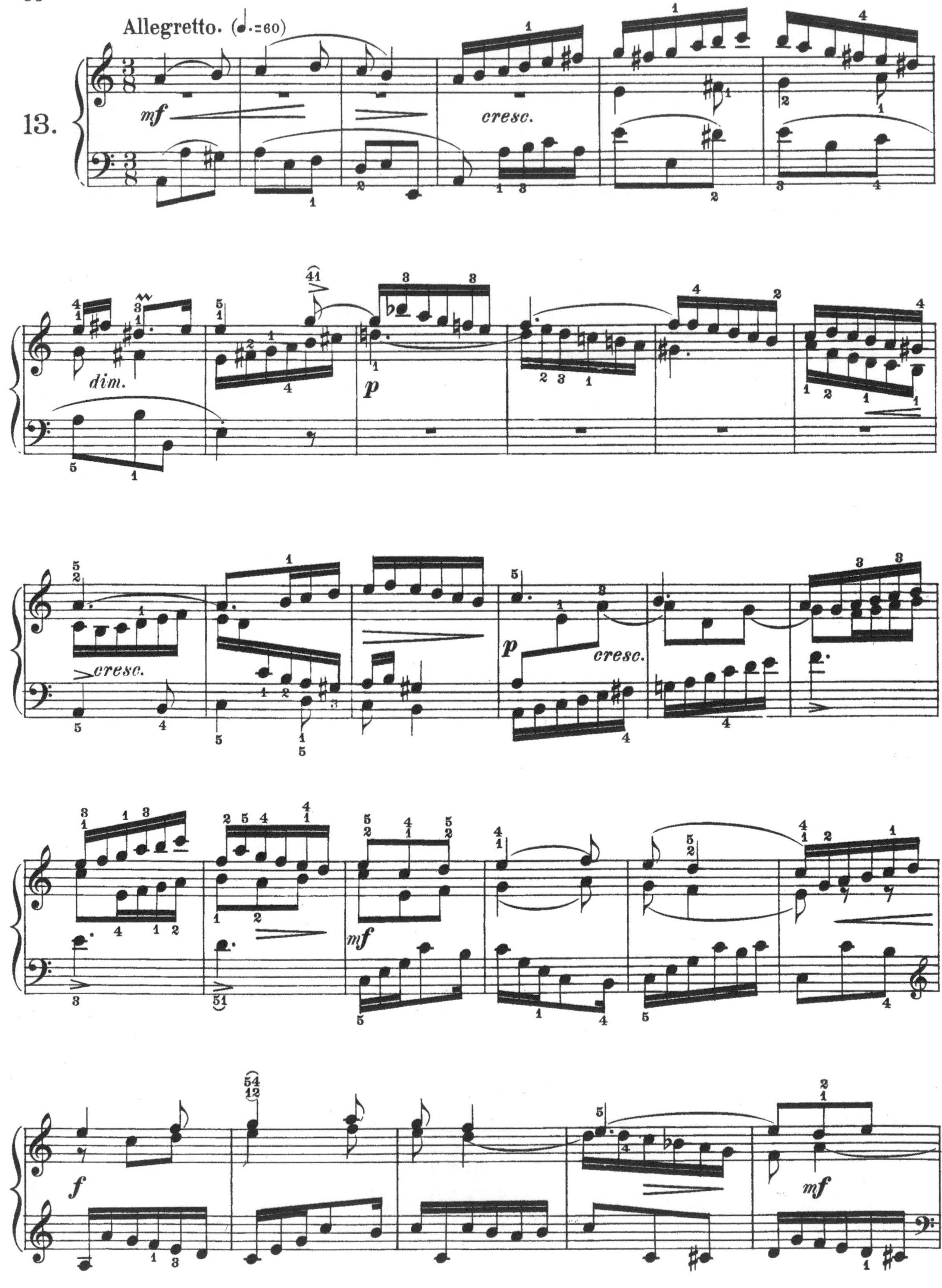
Allegretto. (♩.=60)
13.
mf
cresc.
dim.
p
cresc.
p
cresc.
mf
f
mf

f
dim.
p
poco cresc.
mf
f
dim.
p
cresc.
f

14.
Andante con moto. (♩=66)
p
cresc.
f
dim.
p
cresc.
f

dim.
p
cresc.
f
dim.
p
cresc.
f

Allegro moderato. (♪ = 112)

15.

mf

mf

p

cresc.

f

dim.

p

cresc.
p
cresc. poco a poco
f
mf
cresc.
f
f
mf